A glance back at

Mitcheldean

Mitcheldean from the south around 1910, with the spire of St Michael's church in the centre, and the brewery, George Hotel and the rectory prominent to its right.

by
Paul Mason

Acknowledgements

Thanks for assistance and for the loan of pictures to N. Little, M. Matthews, A. Cottrell, M. Hyett, L. Tuffley, A. & M. Griffiths, T. Cale, M. Lythaby, C. Phelps, R. Hale, C. Mason, R. Wilks, The Archive Shop and Xerox Ltd, Mitcheldean.

North Phen House was the home of solicitor Edwin Yearsley when this view was taken around 1910. It stood on the junction of Abenhall Road, where the Lamb Restaurant is today.

OTHER TITLES IN THIS SERIES

1. A glance back at . . . Lydney *by Neil Parkhouse*
2. A glance back at . . . Lydney Docks *by Neil Parkhouse*
3. A glance back at . . . Bream *by Ruth Proctor Hirst*
4. A glance back at . . . Lydbrook *(in preparation)*
5. A glance back at . . . Coleford *by Keith & June Webb*

for Carol

British Library Cataloguing-in-Publication Data. A catalogue
record for this book is available from the British Library
ISBN 1 903599 01 6

Black Dwarf Publications
47 – 49 High Street, Lydney, Gloucestershire GL15 5DD

Printed by M.D. Jenkins Ltd.,
Unit 53/54, Lydney Trading Estate, Harbour Road, Lydney, Gloucestershire GL15 4EJ

~ A short history of Mitcheldean ~

The parish and the town of Mitcheldean is situated on the very edge of the Forest of Dean, some 10 miles west of the city of Gloucester. Its position at the base of the hills, on the eastern fringe of the modern Forest of Dean boundary, adjacent to the pasture lands beyond, proved an ideal location for a town to develop. Mitcheldean has indeed proof of a very long existence, stretching right back to the Domesday book and almost definitely beyond.

Mitcheldean is one of those communities which is sometimes referred to as a village and sometimes a town. However, it has a town hall and a fairly substantial population which would suggest that it is in fact a town. Though it has always had close links with the communities of Abenhall and Plump Hill, these areas are very definitely separate communities in their own right.

It lies on the route of an ancient road, which stretched from the Roman military road between Gloucester and South Wales, from its junction at Highfield, Lydney. This road passed through Mitcheldean (a distance of just over 10 miles) and probably beyond to Ariconium (Weston-under-Penyard.) However, historians have disagreed about the provenance of the road for many years. Certainly, the present day remains of it are much later than the Roman period. What seems the likely explanation is that it is a later construction following the course of an original Roman route and, being quite narrow, only a minor route at that. It would have been used for carrying iron, made from locally mined and smelted iron ore, out of the Forest to the north. If this was indeed the case, it can probably be assumed that a small settlement would have existed at or near Mitcheldean.

The first definite proof of settlement comes from the Domesday book by mention of Dene, lands totaling 2 hides and 2 1/2 yardlands, held in 1066 by thegns Godric, Elric and Ernui, and in 1086 by William, son of Norman. The estate became known as the Manor of Dean and afterwards as Mitcheldean or Great Dean to distinguish it from nearby Littledean, Michel being the Gloucestershire equivalent of great. Occasionally, the parish has also been referred to as Michael Dean from the dedication of its church, though the modern spelling of Mitcheldean comes from a mistake on the part of the postal authorities, who added the letter 't' despite documentary evidence to the contrary.

The earliest Lords of the Manor were responsible for the woodwardship of the Bailwick of Mitcheldean, paying rent to the St Briavel's Castle estate. The custody of the manor was either purchased or passed down through a succession of heirs and included amongst them are names with which we are familiar today. Names such as Baynham, Colchester and Walwyn have lived on through road naming schemes on the modern housing estates.

The town of Mitcheldean, part of which lay in the neighbouring parish of Abenhall, began to develop into a centre based on the products of the nearby forest and like most other small communities it was mainly self sufficient. The town itself

The Beech Walk, at the Wilderness on Plump Hill, has been a popular beauty spot for generations but unfortunately today has lost much of its former glory. Though a narrow path still exists between the trees, fern, nettles and scrub have replaced much of the grass seen here, which was once kept down by grazing animals.

remained almost unchanged for centuries, with most of the early development taking place around the magnificent church. A charter, granted by Henry VI in 1328, allowed Mitcheldean to hold markets and this attracted not only commodities normally unavailable to the town but also brought influence from visitors.

By 1430, a cross was erected, known as the High Cross, which incorporated a covered area for market traders. This stood in the area known today as 'The Cross'. To the west of the church was a medieval manor house. The town expanded northwards along the High Street, with a new site for the market established by 1431. This market house was known as the Chipping Cross and was rebuilt in the 1760s. Expansion continued from the market house to the fork of the Newent and Ross-on-Wye roads, with that area being referred to as Garons End and later Townsend. Southwards, settlement took place at the Merrin, a cross being erected there by 1411. From the mid 16th century many buildings in the town were rebuilt, more houses and shops being added by infilling. Very few structures in Mitcheldean survive from this time, the best examples being the three timber-framed houses in Millend Street.

An independent church was established at Mitcheldean from around the 1670s, on a site west of Silver Street which at one time passed further east than its present location. The chapel was rebuilt in 1822 and provided with a schoolroom in 1842. In 1850 more extensive alterations were paid for by Samuel Addington of London and towards the end of the century the chapel became known as the Congregational.

Most views of Mitcheldean are dominated by the magnificent church of St Michaels and all Angels and this view of circa 1908 is no exception. It was built of local stone but it is possible that an earlier church of wooden construction once stood on the site. The earliest architecture of the present church dates from the 13th century, though there has been many alterations and renovations since then, including the rebuilding of the 184 foot spire which fell in 1731. In the foreground is the timber yard and steam saw mills owned by George Smith. Today the site is the depot of Cottrell's Coaches.

The earliest school in Mitcheldean was established before 1545 and, as in common with most areas, education was primarily for boys and run by the church. Th school was based in a succession of parish houses until 1784, when charity schools for boys and girls were established. In 1790 the boys' school benefited from William Lane's trust and though the schools shared the same premises, they did not amalgamate until the 1890s. The present school site has been used since 1850, when a new facility was built in the grounds of the rectory. Abenhall and Plump Hill had their own schools, with the former closing in 1904 and Plump Hill in 1984. A senior school for Mitcheldean and adjoining parishes was opened at Abenhall in 1930. It was known as Abenhall Secondary Modern from 1944, and was enlarged and rebuilt at a cost of £105,000 in 1961. It became a comprehensive in 1985, changing its name to Dean Magna School.

By the late 17th century the estate centered on a large house built at the Wilderness by Duncombe Colchester. It was he, too, who laid out the Beech Walk, which stretches from the approach to the Wilderness House to the top of the Stenders Road. It was made from wasteland, the area then being landscaped to give some magnificent views. The parish of Abenhall was separate from the estate and had its own manor house and church. Mitcheldean continued to exist as a small congested market town, mainly self sufficient but with no large industries of its own to support a population of about 500. Instead, the town's menfolk were forced to look for employment elsewhere, mainly in the mines and quarries of the Forest of Dean. Other key industries for the Mitcheldean workforce included agriculture, tanning, cloth making and nail making. The town received its water supply from a reservoir at the Stenders from 1900 and possibly before, and electricity was supplied over the Wilderness by the West Gloucestershire Electric Company from their power station at Lydney from 1923. The town went into a period of decline in the18th century but the expansion of the Forest of Dean coalfield in the 19th century meant many men were able to find employment in this industry.

Comic postcard c1905 extolling some of the attractions of Mitcheldean!

Probably the most instantly recognised buildings in Mitcheldean are the complex of old brewery buildings in the centre of the town. They were built from familiar sandstone blocks quarried from the nearby Wilderness Quarry. The Forest Brewery was founded in 1868 by Thomas Wintle and in due course became the largest brewery in the district employing 60 men. In 1872 the new malthouse was built at Mitcheldean and from about 1893 the business was run by Thomas's son Francis. The brewery's slogan was 'Mitcheldean Ales - Best in the West' and they certainly tried to live up to their reputation by supplying over 170 premises, not only in the Forest but as far afield as Abergavenny, Hereford and Pontypool. In 1923 the business was put up for auction and eventually sold to a consortium headed by Mr Kenyon Homfray, who was once the managing director of Wintle's brewery business. Eventually, the brewery was taken over by The Cheltenham Original Brewery Co Ltd, before finally closing on April 5th 1930. Some of the complex was used for storage after 1930 and the Maltings were leased to Collets of Gloucester until 1945.

The opening of a cement works half way up the Stenders in 1885 was met with an air of anticipation, as the town looked forward to a local employer and the possibility of a large number of reasonably secure jobs. A large crowd and even the Weston Brass Band attended the laying of a foundation stone but this early optimism was soon dampened as the venture struggled from one crisis to another before finally closing in 1914. The man behind the original scheme was Maynard Willoughby Colchester-Wemyss, who owned the Wilderness estate, and limestone at the Stenders was quarried for use in the cement making process.

The 20th century brought about the biggest changes in Mitcheldean's history, largely because of a remarkable coincidence brought about by the Second World War. British Acoustic Films had acquired the old brewery site after national policy had dictated that key firms should move out of London during the Blitz. BAF fell in this category as they had turned to the production of searchlight equipment, gunfire direction tables and film projectors. The original brewery site covered only a few acres. The reconstructed factory was put into operation in 1941, with a group of about 20 men arriving from Shepherds Bush to start up production. Soon local labour began to be employed and by the end of the war the workforce had grown to 250.

In 1948 BAF became part of the Rank Organisation operating as Rank Precision Industries. At around the same time the Haloid Company of Rochester, New York, took out the first license and sponsored the development of the dry copier, the brainchild of American Chester Carlson. Haloid, who later became the Xerox Corporation, signed an agreement with the Rank Organisation to form Rank Xerox in 1956. With the Mitcheldean factory looking to attract new work, the opportunity to build this untried new product represented a big commercial risk but it turned out to be an incredibly successful venture. Demand for the world's first dry copier took off beyond all expectations and at Mitcheldean production soared. As new products were introduced, the Mitcheldean site was expanded time and again with the workforce increasing accordingly. This meant that much more housing was needed in the town and large private housing estates were built to supplement the council housing estates that were developed from 1939.

The centre of Mitcheldean also underwent considerable change during this period, with the majority of the buildings in the High Street being demolished to widen the road and to make way for more modern structures. By the 1970s, the Xerox workforce had reached a staggering 4,700 and these days were described by one former works manager, Mr Don Elliott, as one of the highlights of the industrial history of the west of England. Unfortunately, these days of expansion could not last forever and due to fierce competition from both home and abroad the workforce was trimmed to around 1,000 in 1984. The Xerox Company set up the Xerox Business Park, which included the Mitcheldean Enterprise Workshops (MEWS) centered around the old brewery buildings, which fortuitously have managed to survive all these changes, to attract new business to the site. This again proved a success and much needed alternative employment was brought to the town.

However, in late 2001, after several years of rumour regarding the future of Rank Xerox in the town, the company broke the devastating news that it was to close down its main manufacturing operations in Mitcheldean with the loss of nearly 1,300 jobs. All that will remain is a repair and maintenance facility, and a small specialist manufacturing operation, employing about 250. It is expected that severance settlements will be generous though, so hopefully some will use their payouts to start up small businesses of their own. In the meantime, the Forest is once agin facing a jobs shortage.

Since the introduction of photography the whole area around Mitcheldean, as well as the town itself, has been very well covered and many old postcards in particular have survived. The area has also been fortunate in that several local historians have had the foresight to record the changes that have taken place. It is from this wealth of material that the pictures and text for this look back at Mitcheldean's more recent history have been taken.

Looking from the George car park towards the church, with some demolition in progress in the early 1960s. The town unfortunately lost many of its early buildings during the road widening and improvements carried out at this time.

Two views of Mitcheldean cross, taken from the exact same spot but separated by nearly fifty years. In the top view, taken around 1910 by Will Phillips of Gloucester, Joseph Dawson's general stores, where he worked with his daughter, is featured on the left. Officially described as grocers and drapers, the Dawsons supplied all manner of items to Mitcheldean folk. The church is behind the shop and the church gates can be seen just beyond. The shop on the right is Harness Stores. The view below was taken around 1958. Dawson's are still trading but the shop opposite is now Hardwick's newsagents and general stores. In the early 1960s, Dawson's closed and the three-storeyed building and the cottages nearby were demolished, being replaced by the church garden.

On the west side of the High Street opposite the White Horse stood the Red Lion Inn, which was also known sometimes as the Lion Inn. The Red Lion had occupied this site since 1621and it lasted as a licensed premises until closure in 1922. The Red Lion is open for business in this view, which must therefore have been taken prior to 1922. It shows just how cramped and narrow the High Street was and the baby held in its mother's arms would have witnessed many changes in its lifetime. This view looks southwards down the High Street towards the church and today none of the buildings remain standing. The entrance into Brook Street can just be seen between the flat roofed white building and the taller building just beyond. The large three storey building in the centre of the view once housed a billiards room. In 1936, the Red Lion had a new lease of life when it became one of the earliest Youth Hostels in the country and during the Second World War it was even used as a makeshift cinema. The two late 1950s views left, show it as a Youth Hostel. The building was finally demolished in July 1984 to make way for a small housing association development. This development was undertaken by John James Builders Ltd of Drybrook, who retained the original arch of the Red Lion as a feature of the new development. The new houses of Archway Court were opened by Mrs Edna Healey, wife of the former Chancellor of the Exchequer, in 1990. The lorry in the left background of the middle photograph was owned by Oliver Hail, coal merchant.

The High Street c1920. Owen Staley stands on the right, next to District Nurse Bailey. The children behind them are Cyril and Doris Haile of the Rocks, Plump Hill. Staley ran the general stores opposite, and his shop and store room next door are the only buildings still standing, except for a couple of private houses opposite the Brook Street entrance. The Co-op took over the premises in 1943 and after they moved to their current location in the 1960s, the buildings were converted for their current use as a fast food outlet. The flat roofed white building was George Jones' grocery store and the three storeyed house just beyond had a billiards room on the second floor run by Ernie Jones.

The High Street has changed out of all recognition since this c1958 view was taken, due to the road widening and demolition schemes of the early 1960s. The entrance to Brook Street is in the left foreground. One of the few buildings remaining and instantly recognisable is Voyce's shoe shop at the far end.

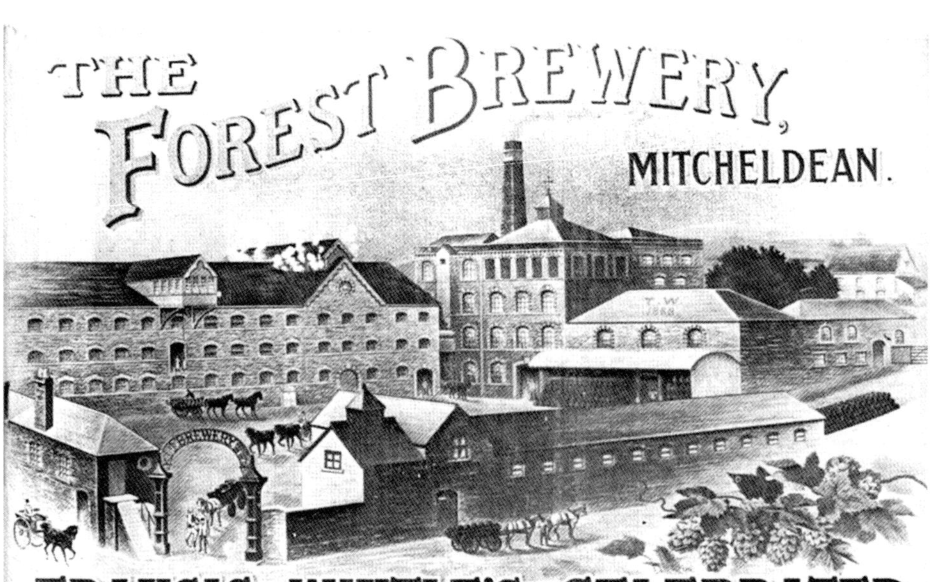

The illustration of Wintle's Brewery, above, was produced as a superb colour poster for display at the many pubs they supplied. The main view below shows the devastation caused by the fire of 1925. The inset view is *Dorothy*, Wintle's Thornycroft undertype steam lorry, used for deliveries around the area.

After Wintle's closed, it was bought by Phipps's Brewery in Northampton and amazingly still survives today in private ownership. The brewery complex was rebuilt and used by Rank Xerox for many years. This magnificent array of buildings is now an industrial park, home to numerous small businesses.

FOREST STEAM MILLS & BREWERY

MITCHELDEAN,

Mr C. G. Baynham May 17 1893.

BOUGHT OF FRANCIS WINTLE,

Brewer, Maltster & Miller.

DEALER IN

HOPS, SEEDS, OATS, PEAS, BEANS, BARLEY, MEAL &c.

ALL CASKS NOT RETURNED WITHIN THREE MONTHS & SACKS WITHIN TWO MONTHS. WILL BE CHARGED FOR.

Above: A group of brewery workers around 1920.

Top: Late 19th century letterhead for Wintle's Forest Steam Mills Brewery, as it was then called.

Telegrams: "Wintle, Mitcheldean."

National Telephone No. 2 Drybrook.

Francis Wintle,

— THE BREWERY, —

MITCHELDEAN, GLOS.

Brewer, Maltster and Miller.

NOTED PALE ALE AND STOUT supplied in casks of any size.

Flour Mills, Cinderford.

All communications should be addressed to—

FRANCIS WINTLE,

The Brewery :: Mitcheldean.

Circa 1910 advertisement for Wintle's Mitcheldean brewery.

Brewery workers from circa 1890 sit proudly for the camera, posed with two delivery wagons owned by Thomas Wintle. The man on the far right appears to be promoting the company's product.

This prize winning specimen looks forlornly into the window of Mason's butchers shop in 1905, as if predicting its fate. Fred Mason was a butcher of notable repute who operated from this shop in Stars Pitch. He also ran a farm at the Wilderness where he had his own slaughterhouse. The premises were later used as a fish and chip shop by Mrs Brookes, then by Mrs Reed and finally by Mr Knight. In 1977 the building became the home of Bailey's Opticians, who used it until they closed in 1999.

On the left of this c1912 view is Carisbrooke House, formerly the Carisbrook Temperance Hotel and before that the White Swan. Proprietor L.A. Baynham is offering Boarding & Posting, accommodation for tourists and cyclists, teas, luncheons and beds. The Town Hall is seen in its original condition before the market place was filled in and the outside stairway removed. Beyond is the White Horse Hotel.

Townsend, in 1906, was literally the end of the town save for a few scattered houses just beyond. The hardware shop on the left was Rudge's; it later became a chemist's run by Henry Thorne. The modern day entrance to Churchill Way is about where the men are stood and the now demolished building, with the stable door, was Smith's the basket makers. Glen Rock house in the far distance still survives and was formerly the police station. The White Horse Hotel was run at this time by B.J. Flooks. York House on the left and the hardware shop were both victims of road widening.

Bradley Court Hotel was situated just outside Mitcheldean, on Bradley Court Road which heads towards Newent. It was originally built as a private house by a Mr Barrett and was known locally as the Mansion. It continued to be used as a private dwelling for many years until an agricultural college was established there between 1908 and 1937, following which it then became the Bradley Court Hotel. The first view dates from around 1925 and shows the exterior of the building when it was still in use as a college. The other two pictures are from a series of interior views of the hotel circa 1958, showing the television lounge and the rather grand entrance hall. These were published as postcards and were available for guests to buy. They turn up quite frequently, proving how popular the hotel was at this period. Indeed, the actress Diana Dors spent her honeymoon here. The hotel closed about 1980 and the building was then converted for its present use as the Forest Court specialist nursing home, providing care for people with dementia.

Television Lounge, Bradley Court Hotel, nr. Mitcheldean. MDN.11

Main Hall and Fireplace, Bradley Court Hotel, nr. Mitcheldean. MDN.12

In 1906, the Chastan Syndicate was formed to mine gold on Lea Bailey, after traces were found in the sandstone rocks which resembled those found in South Africa. Unfortunately, it quickly became clear it only existed in minute quantities and the operation was soon wound down.It seems likely the whole thing was a scam, designed to lure unsuspecting investors. Indeed, it ended with one of the syndicate being prosecuted in the law courts in London, where it was stated that the £1 shares issued to raise capital were at one time trading at £10 each! In 1921 the Bailey Level was driven towards Wigpool in search of iron ore but again this operation was short lived and the entrance sealed. It can still be seen and in recent years Ray Wright has done some work towards opening it as a tourist attraction.The top view shows the entrance to the mine shortly after it opened, middle view, one of the ventilation shafts, and the bottom view shows the surface buildings, together with nearly 30 men, presumably those employed during the mine's construction.

The view from Lea Bailey across to the Lea about 1905, with Mitcheldean Road station sitting neatly in the landscape in between. Note the corn stooks in the field. Although not serving an area of great population, the goods yard was kept busy with milk and agricultural produce going out and machinery, fertiliser and general goods coming in. The tickets, right, are from GWR days, with a first class ticket to Longhope, a child's third class ticket from Ross to Mitcheldean Road and a parcel label.

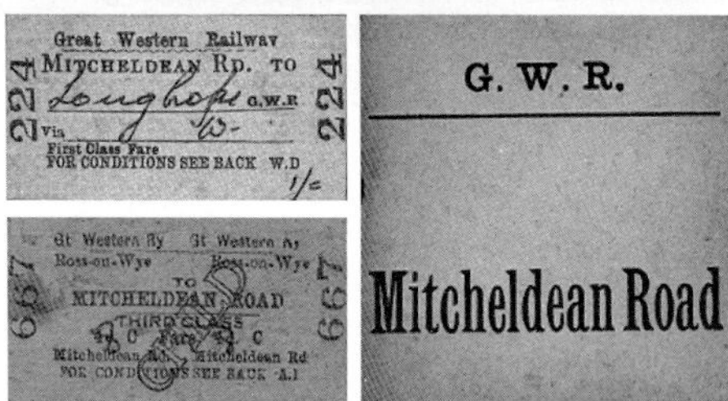

Mitcheldean Road station around 1912, with a pick-up goods from Hereford passing through on its way to Gloucester. The bulk of Lea Bailey Hill rises in the left background. The Hereford,Ross & Gloucester Railway was opened in 1855 and the station was actually situated some $1^1/_2$ miles from Mitcheldean at the Lea but it was the nearest railway station to the town. Adding 'Road' to the name was a common GWR ploy for stations situated nowhere near the towns they purported to serve! The line from Cinderford to Drybrook, built in 1878, was continued on to Mitcheldean Road but it never opened to traffic and most of the rails were removed in 1917. Mitcheldean Road station closed as part of the Beeching plan in 1964 and the site is now covered with by a small housing estate.

Looking up from the Cross c1910, above, towards Stars Pitch. The shops on the left have all disappeared and been replaced by the George car park. The baker's boy and cart are outside the bakery shop run by Mr Rogers and just below was Gable's harness shop. The third shop in the row, nearest to the camera, was Little's sweet shop, who are advertising pop and ices as well as Cadbury's chocolate. Opposite is Voyce's shoe shop, whilst just outside the dog lying in the street knows he is in little danger of being run over save for the occasional pony and trap, one of which is heading in his direction. Below is a similar view dating from around 1930 taken by R.G. Gibbs of Cinderford. Voyce's shop looks much smarter than in the earlier view and there is even less traffic.

The view above is looking down Stars Pitch towards the church in 1909, with a flock of sheep being driven up the street. The left hand side of the street has hardly changed at all but everything on the right has been demolished and replaced by Dunstone Place. The Seven Stars Inn in the left foreground had already closed by the time this view was taken. The children are stood outside Payne's greengrocers and the house to the right of the shop was later the home of Mr Malpas, the Headmaster. Below is a view looking down Hawker Hill c1910, with Bachelors Hall jutting out into the road. The boys are stood beside the Midland Bank, which occupied these premises until around 1976. A large room at the front was used as an office by solicitor Mr Wadeson and later by Mr Yeardsley, who lived further down the hill. Beyond the Rectory wall on the right, the chimney of Mitcheldean School can just be seen. Hawker Hill got its name from an adjoining field called Hockerell (c1640) and by the 18th century was known as Horker Hill, from the Old English '*hocer*' meaning a tump or hill.

A 1905 view looking towards Gloucester Road from New Road, with the Lamb Inn on the right. The large white house on the corner is Forest House, once the home of Francis Wintle. At this time the occupier was Mr W. Wolley, whose wife was a sister of Francis Wintle. Mr Wooley was a typical English gentlemen, always extremely well dressed and often seen in the neighbourhood driving his four-wheeled wagonette. Forest House later became the doctor's surgery, before reverting back to private accommodation in 1983 when a new surgery was opened in the High Street. The Lamb Inn was well known as a meeting place for horse dealers at this time, a volatile bunch who would often end up quarreling in the street after a few drinks. It had also been a drovers' pub, where men driving (on foot) animals bought at market to the farmer who had bought them could stop for the night. The orchard on the left belonged to the Lamb and the animals stayed the night in there. A drover could travel about 10 miles a day.

Mitcheldean. Panoramic View.

The surrounding hills enabled all manner of scenic vistas of the town to be taken and published as postcards, including the two unusual panoramic views seen here. The top one, by Tilley's of Ledbury, is looking from the south-west and covers from Townsend, on the left, round to Tusculum on the right, with Abenhall in the right distance. This was actually sold as one card folded in the centre,

whereas the panorama below is made up of two separate cards, which were lettered 'A' and 'B'. It was the work of the photographer Will Phillips of Gloucester. The view is from the south-east, with the junction of Silver Street and the road up to Plump Hill on the right, whilst the main part of the town is off to the left. The white-painted congregational chapel can be seen facing the road junction.

This late 1970s aerial view emphasises the impact the Xerox factory had on Mitcheldean, covering some 63 acres and almost dwarfing the town. The administration block, in the centre of the picture, is under construction and at this time the plant was at its peak, employing over 4,500 people.

The site was so huge the company even had its own fire station. The pump engine, an early 1950s Commer, is seen here during a training exercise in the 1960s. Note the Rank's badge on its side.

A comparison of production techniques at Rank Xerox. The picture right, c1960, shows the end of the earliest production line at Mitcheldean, where Model 914 copiers were produced at the rate of about 1 per week. The 1990 view, above, shows production of the 5012/14 Desktop copier, which approached 100 per day over two shifts and this was only one of a range of models produced in this huge building. Production levels rose even higher in the 1990s but will finish totally in 2002.

The Mitcheldean Enterprise Workshops were officially opened in November 1984 by Col. Martin Gibbs, Lord Lieutenant of Gloucestershire, standing in for the Duke of Kent whose helicopter was prevented from landing by a blanket of fog. The Duke fulfilled his promise to come at a later date, arriving on Thursday 2 May 1985. He is seen being introduced to Councillor Arthur Cooper (left), chairman of the Forest of Dean Council, by the then chairman of Rank Xerox, Hamish Orr-Ewing.

Looking up Plump Hill from New Road c1910. The white house at the entrance to Silver Street was once the home of the Griffiths family, who were the last nail makers in the village. Their business operated from a shed just across the main road, opposite the house. The business lasted until the early 1900s, having been started by members of the same family in the late 18th century. The premises with the walled garden in front of the Griffiths' house is now the site of Mitcheldean Garage. The last house on the right before Plump Hill was Manor Lodge, a property built from locally produced bricks in 1901. The picture, left, is taken from a similar viewpoint in 1958. Note the lack of trees on the hill.

The Congregational (originally called Independent) chapel around 1910. In the early 1900s the chapel was very well supported, with 40 members and almost 100 children attending the Sunday school regularly. By the 1960s the average attendance was only 12 and in 1977, several years after they had joined the United Reform Church, the chapel was taken over by the Mitcheldean Christian Fellowship.

Abenhall Lodge was built in the 1860s and was originally named Woodville. It is thought to have been built for a solicitor, J.J.G. Borlase, and was constructed from locally quarried stone and given a decoratively tiled roof. This view dates from around 1905, at which time the house had a large garden and some six acres of orchard.

Ferneyfield is one of the principle houses in Abenhall parish and dates from the 1860s. It is situated on the Abenhall Road, about half a mile from the Lamb Inn. Now a guest house, as it was in this late 1950s postcard, Ferneyfield also once boasted a market garden.

Looking back towards the town from Plump Hill in 1958. The white house on the right hand side of the road is Glencoe Cottage and on the left, almost hidden by trees, is The Firs. This road was built by the Forest of Dean Turnpike Trust in 1841 and there was a toll gate situated part way up the hill, adjacent to the junction with the road to Horsepool Bottom. It was amongst the last toll gates to close in the Forest, in 1888, and the house was sold off for £12. It still exists although much enlarged.

A view from the Point, Plump Hill c1950, looking towards the horseshoe bend in the Severn about six miles away. This was a favoured spot of postcard photographers, because of the views across to the river, and this one has positioned two young boys to add human interest to the view. Just in front of them were two pairs of lime kilns, which produced lime mortar and whitewash for the building industry. On the hillside in the background, seemingly perilously close to some of the cottages, can be seen the spoil heaps of the abandoned Westbury Brook iron mine, which closed in 1893.

Also captioned 'From The Point' but in fact looking back at the previous viewpoint, this postcard dates from around 1920. The main road winds its way up the hill and across the centre of the view with the Point Inn prominent on the right. This had opened as a beerhouse by 1851 but was demolished circa 1960 when the road was widened. The limekilms mentioned above are visible on the left.

A familiar site beside the road over Plump Hill was this 'Tin' Chapel, built by the United Methodist church in 1913. It became part of the Methodist Church in 1932, before eventually closing in 1972. This photograph of the building was taken in February 1996 after arsonists had caused a considerable amount of damage to the property, which by this time was in private use. The building was eventually demolished in March 2001.

A rare view of the rear of Plump Hill School c1910 from the Abenhall direction, with Hollybush Cottage just beyond. Plump Hill school was built in Jubilee Road by the Forest of Dean school board in 1878 and included a schoolhouse. Originally attended by about 150 pupils, the numbers began to reduce over the years until 1984, when the decision was made to close. Pupils were transferred to other local schools, most moving to Mitcheldean school. However, the buildings continue to be used for education, as they were taken over by the Wilderness Field Studies centre in 1986.

This rural view is by the Cinderford photographer A. Lindley and dates from around 1908. Houses on the lower slopes of Plump Hill gaze over corn stooks in a field belonging to Church Farm.

The George Hotel, in the centre, is the oldest inn in the town with a history dating back to the early 1600s. In the 19th century, the George's strategic position led to it becoming the principle coaching inn for travellers between Coleford and Gloucester but this importance dwindled with the coming of the railway. This view of the George c1905 shows the building in its original condition with its distinctive pitched roof. The upper storey was deemed unsafe in 1947, and was removed and replaced by a flat roof.

Right: Well known resident Arthur Griffiths holding the Mitcheldean weathercock, which was taken down for repair on 16 January 1983. Several local people took the chance to have their picture taken with it before it was re-installed on 25 April, following a rededication ceremony by the Bishop of Tewkesbury

Below: An unusual aspect of the church, taken from the back of the George Hotel around 1920.

Mill End Street, taken from the cross looking towards Stenders Hill, with Voyce's shoe shop on the left. The photograph dates from around 1905. The name Mill End came into use in the 13th century and referred to a mill which used to operate on the brook running through the churchyard. In 1371, '*Richard atte Mill*' is recorded as being the miller and the mill was in use until the mid 17th century but had been demolished by 1696.

Looking up Mill End Street, showing the old half timbered house in close up around 1910. The house, plus the two buildings beyond it which have internal timber frames, dates from the 16th century. This is one of the few parts of the town dating from that period to escape later redevelopment. The road up to The Stenders was turnpiked in 1769, with a tollgate being provided up the hill and it was through this narrow street that all traffic for the cement works had to negotiate its way.

Mill End looking spick and span (has someone been out with the whitewash?) around 1930. The building to the right of the half timbered house was once the Jovial Colliers public house; it opened in the early part of the 19th century and James Kibble was the landlord in 1885 but it closed around the turn of the century. The building straight ahead at the end was Little's sweet shop, now demolished, and John Cook's cycle shop is on the left, with the enamel advertising sign above.

Walnut Tree Cottage stood in the grounds of a house right on the junction of May Meadow Lane and New Street. The exact date that it ceased to be used for accommodation is not known though it was some time prior to WW2. In 1918, Dave Baldwin, a foreman at the Wigpool iron mine, lived here. This view dates from circa 1920. Today some of the cottage still remains as part of a garage/shed, itself now in a poor state of repair. The large house behind the cottage is May Lawn.

This view captioned Church Corner dates from around 1905 and is looking from the bottom of Stenders Hill towards Mill End; Cook's cycle shop is just past the white cottage. On the right, behind the wall, was the town pound, where stray animals were kept. Stan Price was in charge of it at this time and it cost fourpence to get an animal out. The wall on the left borders Tusculum House.

The Stenders, circa 1910, taken from the church tower, with the cement works in the distance and Tusculum House on the right. The house, which dated from the 17th century, stood in its own grounds, with gardens and orchards stretching down to the churchyard. At this time the house was occupied by Dr Niccol Searancke, who was the Medical Practitioner at Mitcheldean from 1883 to 1931. In the 1920s, it was the home of Thomas Little, proprietor of Mitcheldean Gasworks. The large house in the left foreground is Stenders Cottage and behind that St Michael's Hall can be seen. A former chapel, it was a centre for social activities until it was demolished around 1970 to make way for the Baynham Road Estate. The cement works site is now a small industrial estate.

Tusculum Estate, just off the Stenders Road, had only recently been built when this picture was taken in 1958. The estate occupied the grounds of Tusculum House, which still stands in the centre of this view. It was eventually demolished around 1980 and replaced by four semi-detached houses. The houses to the right are at the entrance to Orchard Close.

Two pictures of the Stenders, from the same viewpoint but looking in opposite directions and both taken around 1910. The local children have come out in force for the view above. The houses on the right, below, called Belmont Terrace, were among the first in the locality to be built from brick produced at the brickworks that was established at Wilderness Quarry in 1885. The last house on the right, with its porch jutting out, was Sherborne House built in 1901. The almshouses on the left were provided by Mrs Henrietta Davies in 1857 and replaced some earlier ones nearer the church that had been demolished. She managed their running and, following her death, an endowment of £1,200 was administered by the Wilderness Charity who continued to manage them up until the 1970s.

The cement works was established in 1885 by the Wilderness Portland Cement Company Ltd but over the years it went through a succession of owners and name changes, until finally being run by British Portland Cement Manufacturers Ltd. At its peak the works, which underwent a major reconstruction in 1907, employed 200 men and produced 60 tons of cement per day. The original intention was to construct a tramway to Mitcheldean Road station and later an aerial ropeway was mooted but neither of these schemes came about so the company's product had to be transported by road to the station. The venture did have its own mineral railway though, to carry stone from the quarry above the Stenders to the works. All power at the works itself was steam driven. Cement manufacture finally ceased for good in 1914 and the site was taken over by the Little family, who ran a sawmills and later a joinery business there until the 1980s, when it became a small industrial estate. The picture above shows cement workers standing in front of the rebuilt works around 1908. The overall view below shows the works in 1910; the chimney was part of the 1907 reconstruction.

A busy scene in the goods yard of Mitcheldean Road station in 1907, with a gas engine for use in the rebuilt cement works being unloaded. The engine came from Paxman's of Colchester and is being hauled off the wagons by a traction engine belonging to Flowers of Ledbury.

The traction engine and its unusual load caused quite a stir on its journey through the village and several locals took the opportunity of being photographed with it and the workmen en route to the works. Presumably, horses and carts were first used to carry the cement to the station for onward transport but the company later used a traction engine and two wagons, possibly as a result of the operation seen here, to haul the bags of cement to Mitcheldean Road. A man with a flag had to walk in front of the engine and horses were kept well away from it. The continual pounding from its heavy wheels and the wagons laden with cement behind, turned the road into a dusty pile of loose stones, which led to many complaints. The traction engine was called *Queen Victoria* and was owned by Mr Read. It is recalled that the journey down the steep Stenders Hill was often eventful to say the least!

Many Mitcheldean men found employment in the iron ore mines from around 1850 to 1900. The principle mines in the area were the Westbury Brook or Edge Hill Mine, the Wigpool Mine and the Fairplay Mine at the Plump. Westbury Brook Mine, top, was sunk in 1837 by the Dowlais Company who continued production until 1893. Total output was 958,000 tons of ore consigned for South Wales. It was sunk to a depth of 666 feet and operated on 4 levels. The man tending his sheep in front of the abandoned Fairplay Mine, middle, would have witnessed a very different scene had he stood there some years prior to this 1920s view. The mine was opened in 1856 and operated to a depth of 805 feet but by the 1870s, like many other Forest iron mines, had fallen victim to the slump in the Iron trade brought about by cheap Spanish imports. The remains of a Cornish Underbeam Engine House can be seen in this view. A short distance south of the pits are the three small reservoirs used for boiler water which today are nature reserves.

The Wigpool Mine, circa 1911. It employed 200 men at its peak, producing 150,000 tons of ore from 1861-1883 and about 4,000 tons annually between 1911-1918. It was operated by the Lydney & Wigpool Iron Ore Company and ore was taken by tramroad via the mine at Edge Hill. Today Pit House (in the background) is all that remains of the surface buildings. Wooden seats were fitted in the mine entrance during the last war and American troops stationed on Wigpool used it as a cinema.

The church as seen from the main road around 1908, top left; respective parts of it date from the 13th, 14th and 15th centuries. Repairs had to be carried out in 1731 when the spire is thought to have fallen down. The gas lamp would have taken its supply from the Mitcheldean Gas Light & Coke Company, which was opened in Brook Street by the Brace family in the 1860s and taken over by Thomas Little in 1907. The view has changed little today, although the graveyard is a lot more crowded and some trees have disappeared. The war memorial has also been positioned here. On the right is a picture of one of the stained glass windows decorated for the 1905 Harvest Festival.

An interior view from the late 1930s shows the Nave with the Chancel beyond and also the WW1 memorial pulpit provided in 1922. It replaced a 15th century pulpit which still remains in the church. Most interior views fail to represent the true size of the church, which has seating for over 500 worshippers.

Pictured outside his home at Number 4 Platt Row is Mr Christopher Cottrell and his wife Annie (nee Foster) with four of their eight children, Arthur, Christina, Alice and Frederick. Christopher and Annie were married in 1883 and two of their grandchildren still live in Platts Row to this day. Christopher Cottrell founded the family transport business around 1886, with a horse drawn wagonette transporting people and goods to Gloucester and back on a Wednesday and Saturday. The business was carried on by his son Frederick, who acquired the company's first motorised vehicle in 1921. The business was gradually expanded to include an extended service to Drybrook and Ruardean. Cottrell's Coaches have built up a reputation for quality and reliability, and the business was extended further to include contracts with schools and businesses, as well as pleasure trips and holidays.

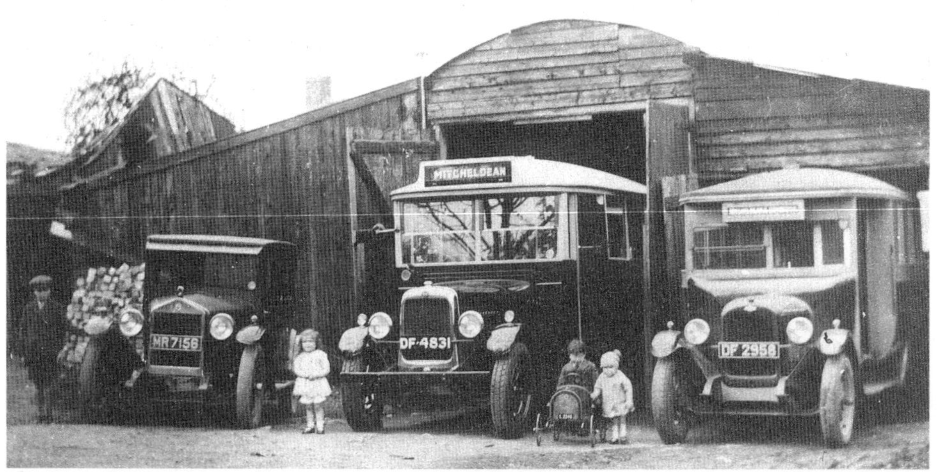

This splendid view of Cottrell's garage was taken around 1930 and shows two of the company's early buses together with an Essex Super Six, one of several cars used. The buses are a 1927 Chevrolet (DF2598) and a GMC T20 (DF4831), a 20-seater dating from 1928. Four of Fred's five children appear in the scene and among them is Bruce (in the pedal car) and standing next to him Edgar. When Fred died in 1969, Bruce and Edgar became joint owners and following Bruce's death in 1998, Edgar has continued in the family business, operating a fleet of 13 coaches and buses.

A number of small transport concerns sprang up in the Forest just after the war, one such undertaking being the general haulage business of C.W. Jackson, who operated from a depot in Court Farm Lane. Cyril Jackson, better known as Harry, owned two lorries mainly carrying farm produce, most notably for the Bulmers factory in Hereford. He later moved to Ross where the business was carried on by his son Ron. This pristine Sentinel Garner was photographed at the works, ready for delivery.

This catch pit was discovered near the Cross when the mains sewer was being laid in the High Street in 1936. Water came down from the Stenders via a leat, part of which is on the right, and it was one of several such pits 'catching' water to supply the town. It is thought the system was built in the 1730s with money left over from the church steeple restoration fund. This pit was rebuilt in Courtfield, as seen here, only to disappear later during improvement works. The man in this 1937 picture is Clerk of the Parish Council Jimmy Barnard and the boy is Neville Little.

Mitcheldean had its own Brass Band by 1843 but it had an inconsistent life and finally packed in just before WW1, the town not having quite the musical tradition of other parts of the Forest. The instruments were shared out between Longhope and Drybrook, with several of the bandsmen also joining these bands. This view dates from c1910. The band are gathered around the base drum which is still in existence today in the safe hands of local historian Les Tuffley.

Successful rugby teams existed at both Mitcheldean (playing at Folly's Pitch) and Plump Hill in the 1890s but following their demise soccer began to take hold. The club began in 1912 and have been a force to be reckoned with since then. This is the 1951-2 Mitcheldean team, winners of the County Junior cup and the N. Gloucester League Premier Division. Back: J. Gregory, A. Smith, A. Cale, C. Little, W. Jones (Secretary), T. Timms. Middle: F. Cottrell (President), M.Stephens, L. Tuffley, F. Tuffley, V. Lark, V. Baggett, R. Smith, T. Knight. Front: C. Loade, W. Brown, D. Timms, C. Byett, J. Phelps.

Sadly the town's cricket team is no more, the team calling it a day soon after the 1988 game celebrating its centenary, records existing of a match against Dymock in 1888. The club moved to the Court field in 1936, courtesy of Mr Wintle, taking with it the large pavillion with flush toilets and veranda which he'd had built for them at their previous ground. It was once a WW1 casualty ward and it lasted until May 1986 when a more modern facility was erected. The old building was demolished by Mr Batt of Chessgrove Farm, Longhope, where part of it survives as a farm shed.

Bibliography

The Victoria History of the County of Gloucester Vol V - The Forest of Dean.	Ed by N.M. Herbert	1996
Memories of Mitcheldean.	F. Boughton.	1974
Memories of Mitcheldean - a study of a Gloucestershire village since 1900.	B.S. Smith.	
St Michael's and All Angels Church, Mitcheldean - History & Guide.		
Rank Xerox Mitcheldean 21st Anniversary Brochure.		
Mitcheldean Cement Works – The New Regard No. 11.	I. Pope	1996
The Forest of Dean Branch Vol 2.	I. Pope & P. Karau	1997
Harris's Forest of Dean Almanac & Directory 1913.		
Slater's Directory of Gloucestershire 1852-3.		